HALFWAY BETWEEN EVERYWHERE

Poems

Copyright © 2022 Kurt Lovelace
All Rights Reserved

First Edition, February 2024
Library of Congress Control Number: 2022942424
ISBN 978-1-953136-04-6   Hardback
ISBN 978-1-953136-17-6   Paperback
ISBN 978-1-953136-47-3   Audiobook

Cover Design by **Moon Song Editions**
Cover Art by Lumezia, licensed from Adobe, Inc
Cover type *Bauhaus Dessau* **Alfarn** by Céline Hurka,
Elia Preuss, Flavia Zimbardi,
Hidetaka Yamasaki, and Luca Pellegrini.
Poetry title and body set in **URW Baskerville**.
Misc. in **Jenson** by Robert Slimbach & **Sabon** by Jan Tschichold.
Flourishes set in Emigre Foundry **Dalliance**, by Frank Heine &
Emigre Foundry **ZeitGuys**, by Bob Aufuldish, Eric Donelan.
Typefaces licensed Adobe, Linotype, & URW GmbH.

"The possibility of man's avoiding self-destruction depends on his realizing before it is too late that what he let loose over Hiroshima, after fiddling with its exterior for three centuries like a mechanical toy, was the forces of his own unconscious mind."

                Owen Barfield
                POETIC DICTION: A STUDY IN MEANING

Poems

- A Cup of Tea ... 1
- Lost in Space ... 2
- Dry Leaves Breaking from the Branches of Memory ... 3
- Lighting-Up ... 4
- Ghazal to Disquietude ... 6
- Litany ... 7
- Halfway Between Everywhere ... 8
- Grading the Weekend ... 10
- Scream ... 12
- Amazing ... 13
- A Few Choice Poulenc Notes ... 14
- Near Closing Time ... 18
- On the Other Side of the Fence ... 19
- Divination ... 20
- Time ... 22
- Everest ... 23
- Vujà dé ... 24
- Brushing Along the Edge ... 25
- French Kiss ... 26
- Midnight Recital ... 27
- Burial of the Dead ... 28
- Like as to the Wind, an Oar ... 29
- Blossoms in the Salt-Sand Waves ... 30
- Schadenfreude ... 38
- A Certain Hesitancy in Tuesday ... 40
- The Boat of Millions of Years ... 41
- The Enumeration of Love, Up to Isomorphism ... 42
- How I Came to Poetry ... 44
- On the Settling of Leaves ... 46

Deranging Ann Carson	47
Cordon Sanitaire	48
Reunion	49
Proximal & Distal	50
San Francisco, 1959	53
Monkey Glands	54
Ad Words	56
Catty-Cornered, Silly You, Even by the Flowers You Bring	57
The Ides of March	58
As a Leaf Breaks from the Branches of Water and Desire	59
Put Some Relish on Your Plate, Pontus Pilate	60
The Day Russell Shorto Said No	62
Barbara	63
Facade of the Well-Lived Life	64
Bouncing the Apple	65
At the Tailer Park in Melbourne, Florida	66
Twilight	67
As I Watch the Opening of a TV Show	68
In The Dark, Shining In	70
House Painting	71
Slippery	72
It Takes Village to Raze a Child	73
Sculpting	74
The Burden of Margot, my Mother	76
Svelte Fat Stains	77
Orphan	78
Hunger	80
Building	81

 Notes About this Collection___83

 Acknowledgments___87

 About the Author_____89

Halfway Between Everywhere

A Cup of Tea

All day in Kyoto a snarky wind
plays hop-scotch with the Fall's
brittle speckles of burnt-orange leaves

that crunch and announce where I walk.
The abbot greets me at the door.
We sit in lotus, cushioned on the floor.

A pot percolates between us. He pours
boiling water over stone-ground matcha,
whisks it a bright green sheen. It smells

like lemongrass split open by Spring rain.
"How much to pour?," he asks. "My cup
holds nothing." He pours, asks "As snow

falls do the shivering birds shout for it
to stop?" "The birds," I say, "Sit
inside themselves until they fall

frozen dead from the bough, riding
the whispers on the whips of the wind
that wraps the Northern lights, pulls them

loosely over the mountains of its shoulders."
He hands me the empty cup
of my hand. We sit and recline

into the emptiness of ourselves.
And we drink.

Lost in Space

I've never felt fully in control of my life.
So unlike Will Robinson, who walks alone
confident in the dark, navigating rocks

jutting up from soil like jagged giants.
Will moves without tripping, welcomes
vast rivers blocking his way ahead

where his cleverness already owns solutions
unfolding from his brain, his small frame
skedaddling across enormous painted

draperies of a B&W planet. Chalk light grows
on slate grass. Black-glass insects ooze
on skin-thin leaves. Undaunted, Will squeezes

his walkie-talkie, hailing Alpha Control.
As if we too could call out, waiting light years
for an answer to find its vast way back

between the vacuum and the stars,
for what is control but the hand's reaching
out, when there's no one there to tell us how,

manipulating, from the rotation
and twisting wheels of the shoulder
the things we love and hate that sit before us.

Dry Leaves Breaking from the Branches of Memory

I remember thirteen. Being
with mom, visiting

Bud Gaskin's sister
sitting in the soft folds

of cancer, her face
damaged from the wrinkles

of pain holding her, her
hand trembling, cold, limp

like an old child's. Marbles
spun from her mouth as she warbled

on about something, then stopped
to breathe. She cried out

in
pain pain pain pain pain.

I hoped that I would not forget her
or to breathe,

walking home around mud puddles
and shadows made of moonshine.

Lighting-Up

When I was just nineteen, I had my head
down low on the ground, fingers fiddling
with fuel rods, gingerly pushing them in
while pulling others out, adjusting the
radius of the ball's overall effect
like a woman inserting a tampon.

Then someone else would check my work and then
someone else would check their work as well in
triplicate, everything got checked three times.
It took a lot of applied rational
intelligence to come up with such dumb
redundant systems. It took pampering

to get it naturally set-up just right.
One day Sargent asked: "Do you'all know where
we is aimed at?" — I raised my hand. He
pointed at me. And I said: "Kraków, Gdańsk,
and Warsaw." — "That is correct. They are all
beautiful places, great food, nice people,"

said Sarg, looking at us, at our faces.
Then I asked him where to go afterwards,
and he looked deep past the dark tree-line,
lit a cigarette, and said: "You'd never
be able to drive far enough off to
make a difference. Light-up a cigarette.

And if you've got whisky in your duffel,
drink and wait a few minutes. You'll never
see the flash, unless they miss by miles but
then the wind and blast will get you moving
upwards into the dust-blooming mushroom.
You know we all just buttons pushing buttons."

Back at the barracks, with a pressure hose,
I'd wash burned gnats off of our truck's headlights.
Hundreds of dried dots would flush from the wide
inner fender wells, burnt bodies flying out
swept up into the air. Afterwards, all that was left
was the tossed-away glow of my dying smoke.

Schwäbisch Gmünd, a nice little German village,
was were we had our HQ and living quarters
while just outside of town, in underground bunkers,
we mated solid fuel rocket stages, ratcheted nukes.
Four million dead in eighteen minutes from
three nuclear rockets, nine months Army training,

it's amazing what twelve kids could accomplish.

Ghazal to Disquietude

I can almost hear, as the waves sweep-in,
a mermaid's susurrations, the cold tips of her lips the water
breaking between my sand-curled toes.

Noise is now everywhere I want to be
without it. Cars swoosh past Galveston beach
roaring their inept monstrous lungs. I can barely

breathe. Or think. Why do trees and blades of every green thing
shudder? Because we are a hyper-intelligent
insidious poison? Cats and dogs cling to us, nudging dread.

Ninety-five percent of a car's energy goes towards simply
moving itself not the passengers. Or rather that's 2,500 pounds
of wastefulness before the crux of tissue steering the steel.

In Hermann Memorial Park a yellow-blue finch tries
to sing but fails in the roar cars shed in their wake
on the I-10 adjoining the beige greenery.

I nod-off under a canker tree. A whale whistles out of its water
spout, breathing. I roll under such plushness, floating with barnacles
and sticky ambergris. So glued are our dream's illogic logic.

I am a sticky carbuncle tearing through the earth's thin breathability.
It's afternoon in Houston. I shower again. I scrunch into a
starched shirt. I rope my throat with a dead worm's shiny excrement.

Litany

See the purple and green crayon alphabet scrawled on yellow sticky notes stapled to tiny Glen Hills cardboard orange juice containers sucked empty by a braid-headed freckled girl named Kizzy Rice-McCarten.

See the cardboard, folded and wax coated, that once held the orange juice within it, was wood that came from somewhere green and quiet with squirrels that stretched out on the upholding limbs sucking towards the sun their green certitude of elm or pine or oak.

See how Kizzy tied together her carton creation with thick pink fuzzy wool string pulled through holes in the juice containers pricked with a three-fifths whittled down number two Venus pencil she over-sharpened while working excited in Miss Thurston's after school art class last Thursday.

See how the wool string grew out of a sheep's skin, that had kept it warm through a snowy Spring, how that wool sprouted, cell upon cell, a protein made from the very grass the sheep was grazing on, from X-ray sun to chlorophyll to sheep's cud chewing transformed to the wiry gray mat of wool dyed pink, now holding aloft 26 spent juice containers wobbling in the wind the whole of our English alphabet.

Halfway Between Everywhere

> *"The price for metaphor is eternal vigilance."*
> Norbert Wiener

Halfway between everywhere one begins to see
everything is the limit of the sum
of all that happens at each intersection.

So why have we now suddenly not the pricks
to spur the sides of our intents with inventions
that move mountains, dam streams, and cook
the air until it burns but not the science
to see within ourselves?

Are our egos the logarithms of our greed?

Sartre, Kierkegaard, Heidegger knew
time. We keep forgetting it wrong.
There's no past, present, future to get to
for we are always here within each second
becoming the next second. We live
where we always are, where we will always be

halfway between everywhere

with no outside, no inside, no place,
no stars that the atoms of ourselves
have not inhabited.

There is no death.

Dancing in a drop, swirling, a tadpole
splashes down the river's rocks and crushed
salt of our bodies, building in the tail
and talons of its sprouting hands
new fingers to grasp and spring upon
the green slender of the shoreline's sedgy grass
where a beetle, with its crust of armor
that flaps, drones in the air, and hovers
unprogrammed by human hands.

Grading the Weekend

Sipping coffee, I grade what one student wrote:
"The surviving fifty rare whooping cranes
with their seven-foot wingspread that propels them
in their annual migration from northern Canada
to the Gulf of Mexico fly unerringly and
swiftly overhead as they migrate southward
using a kind of built-in radar in their search
for winter quarters near Aransas Pass."

Surviving fifty myself, feeling rare and whooping
with my six-foot slouch that propels me nowhere
in my daily migrations from the kitchen to the couch,
I live by the Gulf of Mexico, sleep unerringly and
swiftly, undercover, my dreams migrate southward
using a kind of built-in slinky
in search for vaginal quarters
near my wife's Aransas Pass.

To be surviving melanoma is rare
with its seven wretched drugs I puke, that propels me
out of the gothic hospital to monthly migrations
of chemo; swimming in the Gulf of Mexico, on my back,
I float unerringly and slowly, overheard, the nurses'
whispers migrate southward out of memory,
which is a kind of built-in shit-breeder
when I am in pain and searching for the way out
near the dark rings of Uranus.

But survival is everything rare as whooping
or her pubic hair spread to propel me
in my daily migrations from her coffer to wherever
it is in the Gulf of Mexico I am off to, I unerringly
admit to caring enough to love her but
less than I ought too as I migrate southward
using a kind of built-in stupidity
in my blindly succumbing to what is expected of me,
clearly perfecting it into a fairly fucked life.

Scream

I've heard, ever since I've been a child
asleep in the deep night, a scream

heave over heavy wet clotheslines, catch
in my ears and the neighbors'. We all wake

little lights flicking on like candles
struck on the birthday cake of the large flat

sheets of our houses, now lifting the curtains
of their eyes, as we peep out

looking with our ears to catch a solid
shriek. A small horned-owl hoots, two dogs bark

each at the other or at the quick-flicker
of a bat in porch light. A few hands wave

as curtains close their backs again to sleep.
The next day no one speaks about the dead

woman, nor where from her last words, screaming.

Amazing

I could not get my bearings nor my balls
to line up and move in one direction

as the car flipped over and over and over
one hand on ceiling, one hand on the dash

back rigid, feet pushed into the floorboard.
I saw-heard the broken doll of your neck

snap left, snap right, snap left, snap right, snap left
broken bobble head, then your throat, bloating,

cracked open, wide as a Pez dispenser
lozenge a red plush, shag of arteries.

Thought I saw my left eye with my right eye
fly by, bye-bye, but it was just more

of you than you'd ever cared to show me
from deep inside the colors were amazing.

A Few Choice Poulenc Notes

1st movement: Allegro

Today, they found him,
my co-worker, Marc, still upright, rigorous

at his desk, a glowing spreadsheet of numbers
shrouding his face now quite quiet,

his right hand on the numeric keypad, still
holding the rectal end of money

making money. We fool ourselves to suppose
our preternatural natures predispose us

to butcher the world into little bags
of things to sell to others. Now,

home from the exhausting isostasy
of corporate politics, shifting tectonic plates

like a game of whack-a-mole where for every
fire pushed down a new one props itself

up somewhere else.

2nd movement: Adagio

Do we see us as we truly misbehave,
slipshod, naughty, addicted

to our own duplicitous excesses,
no cheap glossolalia

breezing over the particulars
like a syzygy, an exegesis

of the quotidian floating, mid-
sentence, in a zaftig ineloquence

as I keyboard these words?
I watch the boney articulations

in the tops of my hands, shuffling
in and out of their thin

drawers of skin.

3rd movement: Scherzo

Too often taken for granted, we ferry our feelings
about, between, away from, or towards

the more brittle points in our lives
looking for certitude. Death is the gravamen

of life. But you are redolent. The wet tongue
of my eyes licks the perfect bouncing curves of you

that enthrall me past our bed time. Questions
should never be so short as to be

answerable. Nor should they be so long
as the moon is far away tonight

whispering of changes in the weather
as we trundle headlong forth into the wet

pluvious days of Spring. There's sweet alchemy
afoot in the lunar soaked seashells fluttering

bivalves and muscles spiting water, opening
and closing in the rushed shallows as high-tide

tips the whole earth over, jangling
the proprioceptive motions of my body

this early morning, as I look up at the sky
perfectly even-bellied and lavender.

4th movement: Allegro

Once, we were the upstairs lover's with tongues
tasting, touching. Dégagé lips that deliquesce

over the oeuvre of each other is how lovers
speak to unsettle eternal darkness. Plump,

pregnant jelly-belly, you've become
a zephyr, circulating on tiny puffy toes

about the clothes strewn house. And I fey pray
that these ho-hum hum-drum days will work

their way slowly, but slowly, out of my calendar.
I'll tarry here for awhile. As you lean

forward, I taste the earthen, red-tinged
mahogany of your soul.

Near Closing Time

At Marfreley's Bar in Houston, Texas

In a dim lit mural behind the bar,
two swans amble in front of a plantation.
Its white house lies against the river, lonely

for the cover of trees
that the artist left out, as the rushing water
empties into the dark dandelion breeze

of rewritten histories. I had wanted to see
a single woman, tonight, sitting alone
like me at the bar, looking at their life

as in that landscape of swans swallowing
small sips of whatever they find in front
of them, any parts of a life that might

make sense. Tell me I have done the right things.

On the Other Side of the Fence

is lifelessness. To be here now seeing each
thing from this side is a strange given thing.

For days, a spiky-haired punked-out black orange
caterpillar cottons and installs itself

in the armpit where tree and branch connect.
Rain taps the cymbals and inverted cups

of leaves, leaving their patter and pattern
dinging on the soft leaf of my eardrums.

Thirteen billion years I have been the dust
at my feet, of which I am still composed

but now, walking for the blink of eighty
or ninety years, dust that can talk to dust.

Divination

It started with throwing dirt on the ground,
digging things up, looking at the random
dots and points, discerning patterns in the stars
or the neighing of horses, the slow, swift
chaomancy of clouds, the fluttering
smoke of incense, crystal gazing, how cats
jump or land on the ground, forehead wrinkles,
blowing candles out, the stale necromancy
of talking to the dead, the alluvial drift
of motion and figures in molten metal,
the hieromancy of sharp sacred objects
spurting from the sacrificial offerings
of a soul, or onions, or pedomancy
from the soles of feet or hunches gotten
from the ambulomancy of walking,
counting the knots in umbilical cords,
the throw-about of sticks or rumblings
of stomachs, studying the face and freckles
on the first stranger of a troop that wanders
into the village, the sound, texture and
colors in a long pour of wine, wax
melting or dropped on water, the spasms
of twitching limbs, wet burnt ashes, dreams
hissing from a scramble of eggs, pulling
out entrails, bones as dices, pegomancy
in bubbles rising from a fountain, air
blowing its green motions through the trees,
the crithomancy of cake dough sprinkled
on offered victims, rhythms in the jangling
of keys, how a rooster pecks grains of corn,
fingers following lines in a forehead, salt
spilled on a table, spinning in a circle

until one falls down, the vague outlines
of things seen over one's shoulder, clocks
ticking apart from each other, the nimble
myomancy in the motions of mice, reading
legacies in lips, palms, pebbles, postures
of the possible, bending down to see
wet sappy trails in the conchomancy
of snails, bitterness in the bite of sage,
lunar phases passing through the pillars
of sleep, ripples blowing on the skin of water.

I too now type ancient bright-lit symbols
in Python, or LISP, or C, assembling
in the quick tick of a machine
numbers tallied like dirt tossed on the ground,
combing long binary for the patterns
and kinks in the strands of our existence,

what of it there will be I cannot say.

Time

She, who hasn't touched me in months, asks
would I perhaps take the trash out today
before the blue-green shimmer of the peacocks
flight to roost high in the safe night trees?

I stick my right pinky into cold vodka
and stir. Smoky Kahlúa swirls. Sticky,
I lift out and suck my honeyed finger.
"A moment," I tell her, "in a moment."

Everest

I grasp the impulse that might be driving you
to pity me in some odd way for being flabby and fifty
to your skinny and twenty, but you know, I like most
people stopped aging in my head at twenty-one, the
mental self-image of a nonstop Sid vicious, smiling at
you still trying to figure yourselves out, while we
older folk are done with nothing and wandering
everywhere we still can, asking better questions than
the thin shit we dredged up in our well-spent
grassy laid bare-assed whistling hallelujah youth.
You listen to nothing we say, all day, with piercing eyes
as we watch you climbing our mistakes.

Vujà dé

(upon the death of a long lost love)

When I awoke today, not déjà vu but
vujà dé struck me. Everything's unfamiliar

as the moon's charcoal side. No bright terra cognito.
It was as if I'd had a stroke. I wouldn't know it,

would I? So, I smiled and acted nice. A woman
kissed me hard and kissed me twice. I let her tongue

slide down my throat. I whispered thanks
for the butter toasted bagel she'd made.

I patted the collie's head panting
in my lap. Waved bye to the teenage boy

slackering to catch his school bus. I watched
wind-depetalled roses shimmer in light rain.

Everything is the first time I've seen it.
I'm in a dream that's dreaming without me.

The air in my hand is the only map I hold.

Brushing Along an Edge

At Hippy Hollow, Austin, Texas

It used to be beautiful until people got there
with ideas. I don't know why

a parking lot should cover
the green velvet moss that wrapped

the long slippery slate-stone path to the water
under the thick green sun-spackled trees

that was like walking through golden pollen hovering
inside the vest of a vast leprechaun before opening out

onto a beige pebbled beach of bodies
bobbing naked in the sunned shallows or reclining

like purposeful porpoises that Manet or Seurat
would gladly have painted, hips and breasts,

with delicate French brushstrokes. I decline
the five-dollar asking price and drive on

back to Austin, talking to myself, feeling
like Matthew McConaughey

in a car commercial, alone, and bewildered.

French Kiss

Aliens are orbiting earth, dining
on a dimmed diamond table. Oceans
float in windows the size of walls.

On transparent aluminum toothpicks
hover two lips with tongues, sans mouth, sans face,
sans head, sans bodies — wrapped like bacon

around each other, gingerly pushed through
intact lips as appetizer, the whole
human entrée hoisted up behind it,

anatomy impeccably arranged.

Midnight Recital

Kneeling to untangle my dog's leg from its leash,
how did I get here, walking a pit bull in the dark
under the sour leaves of drought resistant Texas oaks?
How have these years colluded to put me
with a woman who doesn't like to be touched
as if my life were still attached
to a former life, lived in felt robes, kneeling,
questioningly, before God's dead silence?
Why do I sometimes whisper beatitudes in Latin
when grinding roasted coffee beans for breakfast?
Why can't a fuck be just a fuck like breathing
or the necessary forward movement of starlight
entering my eyes from Polaris when I look up?

Why is my life so intertwined that it folds me
into fractal compartments that expand, as if
from each decision, outward, new enclosures grip me
as I venture forward, faster than any logic I can conjure?
Should I kill politicians to address society's wrongs?
Or open a shop and sell cracked imported Chinese
Chia Pets? Or get to the lunar surface to erase
the names of loved ones astronauts left behind?
How can this sticky motion of salt and water
hoisted on these dry branches of bone
discern a purpose, lost among thin pricks of starlight
that amble like ancient animals into the night?

Burial of the Dead

Nobel and bright, each one was a real gas.

Sylvia was the lightest. Pound for pound,
Pound the heaviest. Ashbery I bundled
into a dumpster in the garment district
full of manikins that might have been real
but pronouns kept slipping off them like
snake-oil sold out the back of a wagon.
Creeley got me high on how we jaw words.
Levertov turned decapitated squirrels into
bright tulips fluttering in sheen grass.
Snyder logged his way into high country.
Wright broke into blossom, seeds still settling.
Stevens sold me an insurance policy,
a Humpty-Dumpty way of talking that
obfuscates but delights listening ears
like the tinkling music of urine.
Simic I snuck into a haunted house
ride where a witch spits water in your face
placing him among the 6 million burnt
that live in the air we breath everyday
resultant micro-particles that haunt
memory like a fungus under fingernails
still living on, on the tips of white hands,
hatred. Some things are not forgivable.

Like as to the Wind, an Oar
— *for Stephen Hawking*

"I have given up on getting back
to the stars from where I started from,

but as I am an anachronism, and so
still of some use," said Zeus,

thrumming his fat umbra of thumb
over the sun, he slowly turned himself

towards earth. As even his movements are bound
by the speed of light, people on the ground

got to watch him approach for five or six
minutes before the sky blackened with stars

glowing around his approaching outline.
Zeus had already pocketed our sun

whose non-light was just now vanishing
from the sky, while here and there a few people

fumbled with iPhones or fell down weeping still
praying to the wrong god.

Blossoms in the Salt-Sand Waves

> *"Geswind, geswind, wir hilft dem Kind?"*
> *(The wind! The wind! Who helps the child?)*
> – 1964, 1st Grade German Reader

1

Father says: "We're here
to track the rockets." I am seven. Soon,
one man will walk upon the moon.
The beaches
they go on and on, the water
even more. What
about the man already in the moon?

Floating in my hammock
in our triangled A-frame attic's window,
my eyes open and sweep in
the sand-tufted acres of bruised plums that sway
dúned above the seaweed bedraggled beaches
of waves lashed by ambergris glinting
with turquoise from bright suds in whose bubbling froth
crabs scurry-up into, until the stretched palms
of each wave pauses, stranded
rolls-back their clear hands
on the long wet arms of the waters pulled-back
high up on the sand, that leaves it
shiny and smooth and new,
invites us to play.

At the Shipley brother's cottage, Buddy and I
yank orange coral piled by their dad's rusting Chevy.
It hunkers, helpless in the Bahamian sea-spray.
Scorpions skedaddle, stick-sticky, skitter or scatter
if we let them, but we leave them twitching.

2

I eat a hyacinth. Its wet red lips
flopped or folded open, a sticky witch's door.
My tongue feels the ridges of her floor,
unswept, gritty with the bones of children before
I swallow it, to pocket three gleaming cat's eyes.
Marbles I'd won in a dare
with Buddy Bogus, minutes before

his mother pulls me up by my hair.
Hanging, just off the ground, above the dirt road
her paneled station wagon banged against
from Freeport, with five kids screaming. I'd said,
"Shit!" She slammed the car into dust. Stopped.
Her crooked Christian finger shook, "We

do not swear!" yanked me out the car, fisted
my crew-cut, lifted my brain, an astronaut at T-minus zero
not counting, pushed back by gravity. All around me
the plush jungle listened. I peed in my pants.

And sat on her hat, all the way home, counting
the stars of plumb color or those just coming on:
Ursa Major, Andromeda, Hydra,
Cygnus, Draco, and Vulpecula, the little fox
snout poking out through thin pinpricks of light
slow-turning against one fast satellite of ours.

3

Fridays, my parents rush to the Missile Base to dance
once I fall asleep. But I wake up and run, alone,
outside, crying breathless on the sprinkled grass.

Back in, I pull out the TV's boney on-switch:
a soda jerk on The Twilight Zone tips-up
his black and white hat: his third eye
looks out. Something scratches our screen door.

I pull my head tight under mother's milk sheets
and shiver. "Make it go, make it go, away!" Again,
asleep, I fall into the same sticky hole
night after night, grabbing its furry edges, I keep
slipping over into it, only to slip over into it, again.

4

Some sounds have no feet, like running in a dream
with something chasing behind. As a boy

in the Bahamas, in Freeport, in a wooded area
two older boys forced me to be

naked, and dance for them, my penis
slapping around like a snake in the beak

or eye of some predatory bird. I forget
which one it was that kept me, held

squirming, until I ran screaming
pounding my way past the low palm trees. Power

is holding the thing that does not want you
to rape it into a display to play with,

you'd think. If you could think.
"Those are pearls that were his eyes,

nothing of him that doth fade,"
but suffers.

5

My right ear is dead. When I was three
German measles like dappled freckles

grew in me, killing the nerve. My left ear
still good, at thirteen, I heard pretty well

the unprettiness in my parent's voices as they divorced.
I listened in, in the mosquito bitten dark

roof above the living room window. Then rolled
on my back and swallowed my insignificance

in the drifting milky way above. Now
frogs have started up. A few ducks quack. A splash

might be catfish come to nibble on the stars
tangled in cheap tabloid, suspended on the pond's scum.

My chest makes a soft squelching sound like tossed gravel
sinking-in the decay layer at the ponds pitch black bottom.

6

Just back from Germany, my English all played-out,
Dad tutors me three months at the kitchen table.
Yet I spell everything exactly as it sounds:
"Witch witch wood u bee?" At Saint Mary's Star
Of the Sea, in Freeport, my elementary, the nuns
thought me dyslexic, till someone pointed out
I was trilingual, could recite the Lords Prayer
in Latin: *Pater noster, qui es in caelis,
sanctificetur nomen tuum.* It made the nuns flutter,
holding white habits as if they might take flight,
be the sea foam floating inland on the wind
at noon, when they aired their prayers, the angelus:
Et verbum caro factum est. Et habitavit in nobis.

One morning's milk break, I kissed Sarah
under stiff pines. Sea gulls screeched, and we ran back
caught. Sister Anne ruled my knuckles raw
beating their boney knobs atop her desk.

7

Dad unhands me a fat brochure. Green eyes
glitter from a velvet panther's face. It peers
out, jungle palms fanning its black Stygian felt.
"Let's go," he says, cranking our blue battled Beatle.
For half an hour, we bump the pebbled roads
towards Freeport, to see the Brazilian emerald dealer
in his high shop, tucked away, in an alley of hallways,
going up and down, around corners, til two doors
locked with slapping bolts, open. A chocolate man
unrolls black velvet in a curtained room. One bright light
unshines down. I see how suck the velvet is. He drops
seven hazel stones, their rough edges "Uncut," he says,
"from Santa Muerte." As he lifts one to light it burns
green between blood pumping in the tips of his fingers.

8

My childhood lives in textures on the cratered moon.
I watch from a lawn chair pressed into the shore,
sitting, inside fifty, on the petrol-muddied waters
of a putrid Texas beach. How

did I survive my parent's love?

A pelican barrel-dives into the salt-sand waves.
Exploding upwards, its stretched jaw-bucket spills
tiny fishtails flapping like wings from its mouth.
While somewhere, far-off, deep scared whales
walk their watery mountains, unsponsored, free.

I jump off the porch and walk towards the beach.

A stick bug extends its manifold hands, and
boysenberries ripen under pricking cactus;
in-between driftwood, ashore, a hermit crab
discards its shell, and in the shallows a leopard ray
wiggles underneath the sand, its spotted wings.

Schadenfreude
def. German — to take joy from someone's suffering.

There's a certain joy in watching someone you hate
suffer. Naturally it took a German mind
to cobble together and join the words
schade and freude, joy and suffering. I see

how easily it happened. Helmet, pointed
on head, my great grandfather, Peter Kessel, horse
swaying under him, his rust-red Reitpferd, in
WWI came crushing over a small patch

of forest blossoms he guarded. Yellow
dandelions and white Spring saxifrage
had commandeered his fields with their beauty.
Peter's horse snorted and slowed. Ahead,

what had been hidden in the small heights
of tall grass lay a man sprawled on his back.
Peter dismounted, pushed his polished boot
into the man's side. Jerking and moaning,

the man's left hand zigzagged like a baguette
conducting the breeze. He began to sing.
"C'est la vie." Kneeling, Grandfather,
ungloving his left hand, touched

the man's forehead. "Schade," he said, too bad
– it was schade. His own supplies
meager, he'd been told not to bring
enemy combatants back to camp.

The Frenchman was rotten with fever.
Peter trotted on, leaving him. Without much thought
he'd have shot a crippled horse. Behind him,
the man's cries rose like larks into the meadow.

A Certain Hesitancy in Tuesday

I give everyone in my life enough rope
to do with as they see fit. Tuesday

was wet. "Should we have bothered to vote?,"
I heard. Politics used to be what happened on CNN

in some distant country. In America,
the wages of sin pay enormous dividends

at the top in this geosadistical landscape
of global reployment at ever lower wages.

We live in the lickspittle of so many lives
unwitnessed, unanswered, unserved. Texting, I wait

tethered in line for a hot latte to adorn my hands
at Starbucks, muttering as I pay for my pick-up

before I pick-up my cradled handset at my second job
assembling complaints of failures on a phone line.

On break, looking up into downpour, tearing,
I efface my face in the rain knowing

our whole economy is braided to an abortion
like a Republican handshake before church.

The Boat of Millions of Years

Friday, I'm feeling glum somewhere while out
in public, larking across Rice Boulevard.

Icy rain cones-over the blond rag of my head.
Above the doorframe a pigeon craps. I duck.

My dripping face, a blotched Fuji apple,
slops into Half Price Book's steamed air.

Statued between shelves, I flip the leaves of dead trees.
You stand, toes tipped out from your belly. Legs

widening, you kneel down into a bookcase.
I make you move, slightly. We talk, and are soon

grazing over coffee. Your hand recovers mine.
I squeeze it hard. We grin. You stutter, suggest

we hang at your upstairs loft at the Domain
a few blocks over and around a corner, on a couch

bending over, spread open the bright pink boat
of yourself, head sideways, nestled on a pillow,

the room's ribbed sails of long white curtains flap, pop
open, then stiffen full-bellied into the billowing wind.

The Enumeration of Love, Up to Isomorphism

Whatever made sugarcane sweet made it's bark
bitter to better protect its sustenance,

the gathered rain on those days that it rained,
like the terrible useful things that happen

inside clouds or the uteruses of women,
that dank Darwinian booming, thrashing

husks to spread sweet seeds all over the damp
fertile earth. We are each a surfer

buoyed-up among the waves, leaning
into each second becoming the next second

as our present drifts, adrift on the drifting waves.
Fifty thousand year ago, couples

must have gotten down to particulars:
she wants shelter, he wants a sheath

for his penis: they both work hard
to be together. She bears the brunt

of the future, he the burden
of the present. But tonight, we order

pizza for a rent-a-tub party parked
in our driveway in Boulder, Colorado.

A thick discrete tarp shields neighboring eyes.
Outside at midnight, hot-tubing, we skinny-dip

in the infinite distant starlight that is time.
And recline into the plush hush between words

that look obvious yet are nothing
of the kind but hiding from each other

their true intent, the polished fishbone
of a shiny wish, bubbles on a bar

of wet soap that slips from one's grip.
Can you hear the primal drone, just above

our heads? The black dots of two flys that,
miraculous, hover and copulate in the air?

How I Came to Poetry

Tucked into the sagging rear-end
of a neighborhood of immodest homes,
where I attended Jeb Stuart High School
on Peace Valley Lane, in Falls Church, Virginia

my sophomore year, there was this guy, a senior,
named Ferenc Molnár. "Ferenc, what?", I said.
Classmates whispered he'd gotten perfect SATs.
"Hmm," and I let go of trying to say his name.

That summer at the local library
I found "Ferenc" scrawled in sharp pencil
on the checkout cards of books no one else
but he had deigned to date in years. So I

went to the shelf of the first one Ferenc
had courted, a hard blue Oxford press bound
volume stuffed with English poets.
It opened itself to pencil-lined pages

and landed on Shelly. On the floor, with feet
stretched-out in the library's stacks,
sand began to blow and cover-up
my blue jean legs and leather flip-flops.

Now, the long hair of my face burns
in a blond sun. I see the chiseled sneer,
erect on pedestals of stone, ornate letters
that forewarn what a bad ass their owner was.

My eyes trace the powder and flecks of the tiny
hurled bodies of ancient sea shells that rub-out
all traces of his high-on-himself. I'm left
with wind-thrown sand sticking to itself

in the sky where nothing but nothing else
remains but Shelly's words etched in my brain.

On the Settling of Leaves

Your tongue is not here to taste. Email and texts
are a weak ersatz for your absence. I

inhale you with each perfumed letter. The last
sent, patchouli with the musk of you, wraps itself

around my waist tonight. I breathe hard as the moon
shakes powder from her boney skin. And the bamboo

chimes rattle the breeze like the strung bones
of my own fingers sifting through the thick

peach of your hair. Are we a dream that forgot
itself? When I wake, this bright night coats

our garden in a quiet ashen light
powered by the too-long prolonged vacacny

of your leave that leaves nothing unsettled.

Deranging Ann Carson

Slowly, desires as round as peaches
still bloom in me, in dreams I no longer

ache for what any he lets fatten. I
whisk myself away, to ponder in cities

like Paris, wrap my legs around their hardness
and, sticky with love, stagger there like drunk sailors

French-kissing under bright-calm boulevards of light.
Keats' beauty makes me hapless, no helpless, with its

singular truth. Oh, I still wonder or wander, as I arise
mornings, laden with doubt, about how I should begin

again, the approach to where there's nothing. Yet I see
I'm writing this to be as wrong as possible

about every unfucking imaginable thing,
how human touch stains the garden's white gardenias

turns them bruise-black as we too buckle
and slide back into that same long dark.

Cordon Sanitaire

*def. a line guarded to prevent anyone from leaving
an area infected by a disease and thus spreading it.*

I try to find the line that rhymes with breathing,
but I keep missing it. Clouds are still clouds

and sunset still sets, purple and glandular
as a tongue swallowing itself. My fingers

touch plastic bagged chips on the kitchen counter.
Where did they come from? Perhaps my daughter

bought them when she went, masked and gloved,
a criminal grabbing groceries. I

try to find the line but keep missing it.
I sit on a balcony the wind rocks.

Below, ducks quack in the pond. I wonder
if I should wear my mask to breathe in

this fresh breeze? I try to touch the line
but grasp nothing. I know. I will soon die

if I can not find the cordon sanitaire. Why
does something so small want to love us

like this, to plant itself inside our lungs
to bloom?

Reunion

We all pose goofily for the cameras:
our thin lineaments of skin

stretch out
over the fatuous features of our faces

that contort like tortoises. Then attempt
withdrawal into the shiny imagined

shells of ourselves.

Proximal & Distal

1

the pink of their lips had touched but they had never kissed

2

She thinks she knows where I am standing.
I stand in the daedal and dasein
of my own mind.

As I'm driving from work to meet her,
to get-together, a small nervousness of words
jellies up inside of me like ice in a glass

grows into water as it melts, and the sun
slaps its long last hairs of light on the ground,
blinding the freeway as it sets.

Thinking of what to say is waiting
for a leprechaun of no small magic.
We meet-up.

She stops me beautifully, makes me
take the day's bullets out of my mouth
by putting her lips over mine, as we sit back

of an open convertible parked dark. The half
rotisserie of the Milky Way
turns above us on its singular dark

hole as a dove coos,
crying from a nearby hedgerow,
sounding like a child, hurt

that I cannot reach to tend to. For I too
am stuck on the dark perpetual earth
of our abode, like the green absinthe in a dream.

3

I've stopped trying to make sense of it.

As time clips forward, we walk
into the bulk
obviosity of each day

becoming the next day. I call them
historians who sift gleefully
through their own regrets and desires. Yes,

we are all sad archeologists
of our own lives, bent over
digging in the debris, finding

a tattered photo here, an old shoelace
there, a baby shoe, a filled-out post card
never mailed. Then one snapshot

grabs me from its vast distance:
her bared hips, standing out,
the lozenge of her bright red lips

calling, like Spring, with its dander
and dalliance of dandelions, floating, tickles
my nose, as she becomes again, realized, I can

taste the warm fusty focaccia of her beckoning cunt.

4

My affections are not fungible.

5

We want what we want, not what we need.
How odd is that? And like as to the wind
an oar, even-keeled and well-aged, finger-worn, still
stirring the waters, thrumming the flesh of me,
a minuscule man bobbing on the broad skin
of the rippling sea

I cannot see going another day without love.

San Francisco, 1959

Robinson Jeffers, I love your lithe body
pushing my tongue between your perfect lips

brushing the dense fir of your mustache
to get to your liquid perfect tongue, talent

thrumming in your rising falling fingers
trilling jazz like holding an orgasm

in the soft susurration of pressed lips
touching the stiff white keys of the teeth.

No one saw you dying off that bridge.
I think you sit and write each day somewhere

as if it were your last. Yes, it is late for me
to still be clinging to this earth, so much so

that it hurts as I hold your sapling fingers,
thin and pliable as a birch whip, or the tip

of your tongue, filling-in your delectable
disheveled self, telling me you faked it

as leprechauns of much ingenuity
inveigle into a room their bespoke utterances

fooling everyone.

Monkey Glands

Mother's lips were always moist
and wet with products
from Maybelline, one of which

was centrifugal butt gland oil
from a herbaceous monkey
— they did that back then

in the 1950's — for beauty
they would go
to any length of death

to look pretty
for their scotched-up husbands.
Even as if to their own funerals,

half-beaten to zombies, yet
correctly covered
everywhere in a perfect shade

of rouge, their lips, wet-like
parted
to show that false hint,

tint to the entrance
of love and grief, whose silly
labial flaps, colored

like Helen's rose-covered bruises
that burnt the topless towers of ilium — what
was it for his body,

overextending itself
for pleasure? How else
does war and madness

happen?

Ad Words

Who put the potage into sabotage or
looniness in the lunacy of the moon,
the foot upon the shore in arrival,
the mortuary of mortality in being mortal,
the outside-in and the inside-out in the
implicit and explicit in complicit, all
the varying vines that sprout up the trellis
of rhetoric's thick tapestry of words
that tickle the elozable and flattery prone ears
in the echo-centric chambers that are Facebook,
but poets?

Catty-Cornered, Silly You,
Even by the Flowers You Bring

for Hugh Walthall

"A few bulgar Bulgarians are hiding
　in those icy hedges, their wrists,
　　though filled with radio-scopes pointed our way,

will not wrest from me my wistfulness," says Hugh,
counter-punctually slapping at fat snow flakes falling.
He and I trudge thick drifts to enter

the facility, to take down a woman's last will
and testament, being a parcel of paralegals. But
the interview does not go well. Her husband's

been dead for years. Was that what she meant
when she said he's 'often absent'?
Sighing, we lean back. The recording still recording

for the record, she states, "There is no distance
I can travel that will bring him back
from the stars from where we started from,

but to be going back, out there, myself
is the only way. My rooms are now filled
with nothing but a darkening retinue and zoo

of the growing antiques of my life, lived. And yes,
I yell at both of you for bringing me a yellowing shout
of carnations that look too happy to understand

the difference in the spittle between hospice and hospital."

The Ides of March

As the sun wears itself down into dusk,
our old peacock

slowly wriggles his long surreal heavy feathers
showing them off by shimmering them

against the torn pink tissues of the sky.
Today is March 15th and the full throat of the moon

blooms toxic above the the greasy bulbs of tulips
shouting back of the dark creek. Caesar

is dead. They stabbed him
who claimed to love him. But

he couldn't have kept it up much longer,
the old goat. He was like the battery

in my knock-off watch. Dead, I still wear it.
It's weight bobbing on my wrist is a small

constant reminder that by doing nothing
twice a day something about me will still be

correct. I mean how honest can anyone
be anymore in America when we are

purchasing zombies thrown over our car's
hoods, bent-over by corporations, our

incorporate days look like an anal rape?

As a Leaf Breaks from the Branches
of Water and Desire

All-day I've been filtering, trudging to make sense
from one phone call between three text messages

and an e-mail. After a red light turns green,
someone honks to remind me to go on

car slipping slightly on the slightly oily road,
anointed as drops sprinkle. I turn on my wipers.

Switch-swatch, switch-swatch, switch-swatch rub of rubber
blades brandishing the thin rain makes shadows

quick-shifting like sunlight through leaves, in the glass
and streams running their murky water over

the vales and rivulets of my unreflecting face.
Are there any possibilities left?

I write this as if to say, "We have arrived
in the New World, unscathed by the old ways

of turning a phrase" as we turn our bodies
away from each other, always returning

to the schlock disappointments cluttering
our nominal lives where, again,

everything is possible.

Put Some Relish on Your Plate, Pontus Pilate

I started out believing
in everything, the open field,
plow in hand, horse

waiting to be worked, words
hedged in the furrow, irises
open to the moment of opening

as if posturing a proof
were proof enough, but without
the heavy lifting of burdens,

the concrete blunders
one must make, clearing the way
to ubiquitous insight.

If only my own desires would stop
helping the scrunched imp
of all my days rolled-up

into aphasias of dreaming
that stream down like drops of sunlight
through the wet branches of Spring,

it might be enough. Perhaps
I may ask you about it,
someday, and you will tell me

everything I've every wanted
was within reach, if only I had put out
my hands, wide palms like bells ringing,

that clap at a wedding, a wake or
fold in praise at the hours and minutes
granted us. Put your fears in a little box

and smoke them, along with this warm
interrogatory weather we've been having
that peels shirts from bodies with an utter unconcern

that is neither here nor there.

The Day Russell Shorto Said No

Feverish, sneakers in snow, I walked my wet way
across George Washington's campus in Foggy Bottom

to Russ's mid-campus apartment, knocking his door,
fully expecting to be let in. Russ was busy

cocked his head sideways, "I can't,"
he said, "engrossed in a long paper on the *Human*

*aspects implicit in the structure of Heidigeger's Dasein
as an organic extension of Husserl's Phenomenology,"*

and left me dripping the grimy hall floor
before I'd explained my presence,

sick in the dim light. Quivering
plucked strings quavered in the air

their delicate quilted lace, a classic sonata,
from two doors down, where lived a casual friend I knew

by laughter and his grassy laid-back ways. It was
Jordi, that day I had fever, and my body

came trembling at his door, unable
to care for itself. He wrapped my sickness

in quilts, comforted me with warm chamomile
while I rested days on his couch,

uncomplaining as he played, fingering
like a fine wine or a warm woman

the curves of his Spanish guitar.

Barbara

Naturally, we fucked like rabid dogs then
slept. The artist-barkeep who always had a key
to my place, who came at night, politely

showering before slipping me into herself,
kept Shakespeare's plays in the fridge,
cold morsels to be sucked on

and Gravity's Rainbow floating in the tub
with Melville, whose meanings drifted off the page
awash in the spumy suds between her legs,

arose late mornings, and naked, her petite hands
brushed overripe sunsets like swollen tongues
onto blank canvass, stroking them thick fat colors.

Facade of the Well-Lived Life

Teatime with his penis and her vagina,
larded creameries stepping forward to take

each other hither by the crown of their
uproarious gonads, stretching legs

out long until they recline once more, back
into the land of twinkle toes, like fraught toys

floating naked over each other. Now, it's marzipan
madness amid a Kris crinkle candy cane lane laden

Christmas tree. Let's park it in the parlor
and get it dusted with fake snowflakes.

We lie to the children, about Santa, about
debts, about our great loves concealed even from

ourselves, how in a neighboring cart
cherry tomatoes look like detached lips

awaiting ransom.

Bouncing the Apple

Is the penis a muscle? If so, how
should it be served? Isn't it soft, mostly

useless, pulled-out and stringy when ripped
from the shell of a sheltering vagina,

a venomous snake waiting to strike again?
Was that what Eve was holding when she sank

jugular teeth into the bright crisp apple,
juices running down her mouth and in her hand,

one nourishing, the other dangerous
tadpoles to her purpose, her being?

Was it for
her necessary reckless surge towards life,

eating, that she urged knowledge into herself?

At the Trailer Park in Melbourne, Florida

What I leave out is almost everything.
The rusty nail I shoved-up my right foot
dashing through a grassy lot of wood boards
strewn from some left-over construction

that ended my playtime, limping in a sneaker
full of blood crying to a tetanus shot.

But across the railroad tracks behind the trailers,
the dark flayed skin of an equally young boy
whimpered as alcohol dabbed his deep cuts,
his face screwed up in imperfect agony.

Twilight

In the middle and join of mirrored trees
and Rorschach of a lake reflected sky,

a bird flying over its inverted self
becomes lips of a cloud-shaped woman's face

Cheshired between the crease where liquid and air
merge skeletal veins that fractal out

into arteries that trunk from leafed and leafless trees,
where sky cannot tell itself from water

nor water from sky: it Eschers in our eyes
as Earth, seen from an astronaut in space

floats without up or down, no telltale sign
to tell us how it is we've gotten here

where we see only our own perplexity
stems from the well-intention and damage

of dreams guiding our hands that have wrought
this world with the throw-aways and plastic

conveniences for our lives, today, swapped
and traded like water mirrors sky, conjoined

twins moving in dead directions, breathing
the unsweet ruin of ourselves, we frown

in this turquoise twilight that's neither day
nor night, yet ample enough for the end.

As I Watch the Opening of a TV Show

The old doctor scrawls chalk on a blackboard:
♂ man, ♀ woman, ✳ birth, † death, ∞ infinity.

Slowly, he enunciates each symbol.
Such things ought to be less unknown,

acknowledged, discussed with awe and disgust,
factual as gravity pulls a falling body

crushed to the ground. All our lives men
are basically dickheads, slaves to their hormonal

urge to procreate. So in what sense are women
too slaves, ancillary to their uterus?

And what if they meat and make a baby
gurgling, defenseless, soft, blubbery

costly bundle to be cared for, ever
precious and human, meant to out-step us

into the unknowable days long past
our own coffinless decease, high waters

sloshing below a cloudless sun with rare
arctic air, barely breathable; while in the boiling

tropics no life thrives but mammoth sharks
that circle whatever else will swim in those

inhuman waters. As I look up, flash back
to the show, I am that patient, gurneyed

on the stretcher, seeing only the ceiling's
long white incandescent lights flipping past

as I am rushed into a masked room
full of surgery and my own last

thin gaspings, relieved to have lived here now
ashamed at what little's left that we leave

our children.

In The Dark, Shining In

Standing near you, my venereal friend,
I feel vegetable: a vehement vehicle

fueled to loathing at my own vicissitudes
dribbled from the flaccid vibrato

of a lusting moment rent in your company.
Was it a feel-good sham we had, in fun

and sun, while beaching in Rio drunk with tourists
crashing tables of menus like tablets

with commandments etched in fineprint, telling us
what might happen in the near or distant future

if we mix things up, priorities with wants
like fruity dreams stemming, but sweetly as

at the end of a long contract of dry years
waiting, for you to be, as I imagined?

Who now rubs the rich velvet duplicity of self
arranging and rearranging things

as they could never ever be?

House Painting

How now to make ready the nursery?
Preparation always lead to questions. First

we have to pencil-in boundaries and
lineations of animals stalking. Then color them

bright on the white nursery walls. Cartoons
gift children their first taste

of fear, before they wander out
into the blood and stringy gristle

of the gritty world. With cycles
of lifetimes of birth and death,

as the Tibetan Buddhists teach,
"Everyone was once your mother." So

how can we harm our own maternity
now planted on this planet and not be

harming ourselves? I don't think about it.
Brushstroke after brushstroke after brushstroke,

I know. I paint the burning tigers bright.

Slippery

I stumble. My hand catches,
holds your wet

mildewed headstone.
Icy rain

robes me. Its flakes
anoint this lightless mourning.

Now
underneath me

you grow, shine
lucid in the translucent

mold of me. My skin
prickles

wanting the warm
slip

of your tongue in my mouth.

It Takes a Village to Raze a Child

Putrid sunlight seeps through thin
peeled gossamers of skin, floating, delicate
on a soft wind that catches it like cobwebs
on the high razor grass and the thorned bushes
made thick by the bodies meating in the village
still crisping. The U. N. observer snaps
precocious photos that are our self-portraits

burning.

Sculpting

The cost of involvement is you get involved
and there she is
and you're her painting garden her kitchen things
on her desk at the office

and she's looking how it's all arranged
your colors the smell of your herbs
why your dishes aren't put away are your pencils
sharpened

then she sees
carrots need planting, the rhubarb
must go, suddenly
you need new dishes.

Then you start drunk serious writing poems about
the cost of involvement
how her lips are not cherries but
red angry commandments painted in a delightful rouge
to elicit your obeisance

so softly
her requests patter
and when her such and such of such words fall
your obeisance
yawns lifts up its arms at her
smiling

she sculpts you

one night reads your poems and thinks that they are very pretty

But you are drunk and serious.
You keep the gun in the drawer.

The Burden of Margot, my Mother

The grandmother bitches.
And bitches. AND BITCHES.

This may be normal. She may hate herself.
I don't know. But she baby-sits,

sitting on her lower self-portion of her body,
my two little half-sisters, feeding them

lies breakfast, lunch, dinner while my mother
waits tables, takes the bus, buys the groceries,

washes cloths while her husband, my stepfather,
feet comfortably proped-up on the coffee table

reads books these last six months.

Svelte Fat Stains

I want to shoot myself happy, amazed
or awake enough to see new rain

wash through the canal's shoveled arteries
that feed the dense veins of droughted trees,

their wet heartbeats, the dead wood boards thumping
in the wind-rotten holes of a fence's nails

torn loose, through whose prick-hairy fingering gap
I squeeze into, to be with you, questioning

whether that dead calm beatific smile
you wear as a heroine might achieve

is real or fabricated, aided
by traces of lingering heroin

that's still shipwrecking you, a sailor or
assailant to whom I've come, yet again

to break time with like the sacrament, dry
before wine peels away our wet delicious sins.

Orphan

Cut me up, mother-love,
and bandage me with broken glass; eat

acid kisses in my cheeks; rub me red
with the cut off end of a pig's ear.

Clear acid hate. Glass-like, fragile,
I contain it; its fumey words

come up my throat like vomit:
the name of that faceless Father

who bastarded me, and the first part of yours,
Mother, who orphaned me at birth,

left me in homes until I was let loose
eighteen and hazy. If I had your address

I'd send you my hates' kisses ---
the adverse perfection of their silver lips,

kidnapper's pliers yanking off the victim's nose --
sending them, stamped and enveloped, P.S.-ed

I mean business. Mother
who are you? I only have a photo

in which your soft girl's body
flaps in an orange dime-store dress,

and your indistinct face
is a fingerprint smudge on a window.

I've been trying to find you
fourteen years, frustrated so

beyond what the word means that
killing's what's become of what was once

anxious curiosity, and is now
the dark stuff I love you with.

Nights, in dream, I find you.
I forgive you; I puncture you

with guilt until the you in me, approaching,
meets in the middle,

bending with your being there my forgiveness
and my hate into something normal,

into the *"I love you"* in movies, but
more ordinary, less silver-screened.

In the morning it tastes sugarless but covers-up
the not knowing tension of who I am

I bury another body in the basement.

Hunger

Money,
a small quantity of it
jingles in my pocket.

I pass a man on the street,
his mouth
open,

his belt about his waist
pulled tight.
His hand reaches out to me

shriveled. I pause.
Reaching into my pocket,
pulling out a dollar,

and leaning my mouth toward the man's left ear
whisper, I wish you were a
woman.

Building

Eating a wrapperd lunch,
looking at the office building
across the street,

I watch a bird
die into the first story
of its reflection.

Falling, it intimates to me
the terribly intimate stupidity
of the engineer

who flowered the foresight
that birds might mistake themselves
for their reflections

but the engineer who nevertheless
got up every morning and shaved money
from the budget of his building

now grows his dead birds on the pavement.

Notes About this Collection

The Poems

Towards the end of this volume appear several very early poems. There was originally the idea of having a "juvenilia" section, but I was quietly and quickly talked out of doing that.

The last poem in this collection, *Building,* is the first serious poem that I wrote at seventeen, and published in **Wooden Teeth,** a literary journal of the George Washington University. Likewise, *Orphan, Sculpting, The Burden of Margot my Mother, Svelte Fat Stains, Hunger, How I Came to Poetry, In The Dark, Shining In* were all written between the ages of 17 and 20 while I lived in Washington D.C.

Therefore, the poem *Orphan*, for example, may be placed right into the period of the emergence of the **New Wave** and **Punk** music scene during the early 1980s, as occasionally I attempted to write fledgling lyrics for now long defunct local D.C. bands that performed at the **CLUB 9:30**, such as Rodney Franz's **The Urban Verbs.** *Orphan,* in fact, "sounds" like a Punk or New Wave lyric from that period. Context is everything, as they say.

About one-third of the other poems were written in the intervening years, between 1983 and 2010.

The rest, being recent poems, were written between 2010 onward when I studied poetry writing with Tony Hoagland, Kevin Prufer, Martha Serpas, Michael Sofranko, Joy Priest and creative non-fiction writing with Peter Turchi.

The Translations

In Neruda's *Árbol*, my overriding goal was in how to convey the playfulness present in the last line—where *ojos*, eyes and *hojas*, leaves—play off of one another, in the original Spanish. A simple synecdoche, substituting part for whole, so that lashes is used to imply eyes, solves this problem nicely. Lashes even supplies an image of the shape of the eyelid being like that of a leaf. This gives us back some of the magic in the original.

Rilke's *Herbsttag* starts out with a plea for summer to not yet be at an end. It is full of lush imagery that echo's portions of John Keats's *To Autumn*. But, unlike the Romantic era poem, suddenly Rilke transitions into a modernist vein, invoking the harsh reality of what lies ahead, if one has not already built and prepared for what one needs in the Fall and eventual Winter and endpoint of life.

In Jacques Prevert's *Déjeuner du matin*, he appears to use the most direct, everyday spoken French possible. But then, in the last nine lines, we find that even when one uses basic, everyday language, surprise takes hold—and Prevert appears, as though without effort, to produce dramatic puns using the word for rain and tears that, in French, sound alike.

There are no easy English equivalents for this wordplay. So, I took the word 'rain' and extended it metaphorically, with license here, to force a dramatic "play" on this word, and introduce a line that is not present in Prevert's original, while still trying to, overall, bend it to fidelity.

Now, as to Goethe's *Auf dem See*, there is one immediate structural item to note. Goethe's final version of this poem is most often printed in three stanzas: the first, eight lines, then a four-line stanza, and finally again a concluding eight-line stanza.

I will not get into the subtilties of why this makes the poem "go faster" and gives it somewhat a more compact, yet different feel in the German original, other than to say that, yes, it is subtly different. It is also how Goethe originally wrote it. However, it is often broken up into quatrains, as I have done here.

My translation takes one liberty with the last line. I perform a hopefully essential "interpretation" of what *"die reifende Frucht"* might mean, by adding "of ourselves" to the concluding line. For me, in the original German, this connotation is implied, as what else are we looking at besides reflections of fruit ripening on trees but the ripening fruit of ourselves as seen in our own reflections?

I assume that some contemporary English readers may leave it at "ripe fruit" hanging on trees, and entirely miss the deeper possibilities being so economically expressed by Goethe.

This reminds me of the situation with William Blake's poem *The Tyger* where if one treats it literally, then one looses the poem entirely. Most likely, my two additional words will be taken as a too obvious finger crudely pointing backward at the fruit ripening, rather than as an intended, helpful clarification.

But I believe busy readers are in trouble approximately fifty percent of the time, whether they know it or else choose not to acknowledge it—they may need help.

The last translation, of Gaius Iulius Hyginus's *Fabulae*, is one of my favorite creation myths. And I came to it in a very roundabout way. When I first read Martin Heidegger's magnum opus *Zein und Zeit* in my twenties, I came on Hyginus's Latin text of *Fabulae*, and fell in love with it.

But when I went to seek Heidegger's original Latin source, to see if there was more of the story and to read more of Hyginus's work, I found Heidegger did not have the correct version. He obtained his Latin version from another author, Bücheler. Bücheler's version is essentially correct but not the exact text. So, Heidegger's version is a Latin paraphrase of the original Latin text by Hyginus.

The version I translate is Hyginus's original text. The rabbit hole of scholarly minutia in trailing this oddity goes deeper still, but I will leave that to inquisitive readers.

The Essays

These require no explanation, other than that I find it useful to add in-line quotes from an author taken out of interviews or their own essays. This provides a deeper sense of the poetic sensibility and lived viewpoints, from the writer, in their own words.

Kurt Lovelace
Thursday 1 February 2024

Acknowledgments

I would like to thank the following publications in which these poems first appeared:

"**Midnight Recital**" first appeared in
The Lascaux Review (*Jul 30, 2012*).

"**Divination**" first appeared in
Red Orge Review (*August, 2022*).

"**Burial of the Dead**" first appeared in
North Dakota Quarterly (*December, 2022*).

All original poems that appear in the translation section are either in the public domain or else academic fair use, as they are both fully attributed and proportionally short pieces, and are meant only to serve as a sample of the author's academic literary translations.

Likewise, all quotations and extracts and excerpts of original poetry in the essays are academic fair use, as none are printed "stand-alone" and are fully attributed and quoted within the context of a critical literary analysis.

Kurt Lovelace

Kurt Lovelace

An editor, writer, translator, and mathematician, Kurt's work has appeared in **The Lascaux Review**, **North Dakota Quarterly**, **San Antonio Review**, U.K. Lancaster University's **Red Orge Review**, U.H. Honor College's **Athena** and other journals.

Halfway Between Everywhere is Kurt's most recent collection of poetry, where the hardback edition includes additional selected translations, and essays. Two new collections, **Apophrades & Intrepitudes** and **Disfigurements**, are both in progress and forthcoming.

www.ingramcontent.com/pod-product-compliance
Lightning Source LLC
Chambersburg PA
CBHW060544080526
44586CB00012B/855